W9-AQZ-637

Mind Teasers

FUN AND GAMES

Published By
Capstone Press, Inc.
Mankato, Minnesota USA

j031.02
FUN

1

CIP
LIBRARY OF CONGRESS CATALOGING IN
PUBLICATION DATA

Ripley's believe it or not! mind teasers--fun and games.

        p. cm.

        Summary: A collection of surprising facts about games, hobbies, sports, movie stars, music and dance.

        ISBN 1-56065-062-1:
        1. Curiosities and wonders--Juvenile literature. [1. Curiosities and wonders.] I. Title: Fun and games.
        AG243.R46   1991
        031.02--dc20   91-19901
                                         CIP
                                         AC

Color Illustrations by Carol J. Stott

VanCrest C

This edition published by Capstone Press, Inc. Box 669 Mankato, MN 56001. Printed in the United States of America.

CAPSTONE PRESS
Box 669, Mankato, MN 56001

CONTENTS

Introduction

The man that created Ripley's Believe It or Not! was Robert L. Ripley. Ripley grew up in Santa Rosa, California. His two main interests throughout his youth were drawing and sports. By the time he was 25, Ripley was working in New York for the Globe as a sports illustrator.

One day, when Ripley needed to fill space in the newspaper, he found a scrapbook with unusual achievements in sports in his files. He drew illustrations for 9 of these and titled the art "Champs and Chumps." Ripley's editor retitled the work "Believe It or Not!" This was published on December 19, 1918. The column was so popular that "Believe It or Not!" was set up as a regular weekly column. It was not long before it was a daily cartoon.

In 1929, Ripley was one of the top cartoonists in the country. His Believe It or Not! feature was one of the hottest columns in the newspaper. He had also published a book and was now anxious to search for new material. For the next few years he traveled thousands of miles. He visited 198 different countries. At first he returned with many souvenirs of personal interest. Soon, he started returning with huge crates of curiosities. His friends encouraged him to put his treasures on public display.

Ripley's first display was in 1933 at Chicago's Century of Progress Exposition. In two seasons 2,470,739 people lined up to see his incredible treasures. Now Ripley was in demand on the lecture circuit. Next came movies, a top-rated radio show, more books and finally television. By 1940, Ripley had three "Odditoriums" running simultaneously - one at the Golden Gate International Exposition in San Francisco, California; one at the World's Fair at Flushing Meadows, New York; and another on Broadway in New York City. A number of trailer shows toured the country. Ripley was very famous by the time of his death in 1949.

The information included in this special Mind Teaser Edition is from original Ripley's Believe It or Not! amazing archives of cartoons.

BOB HOKE OF SCOTTSDALE, AZ, USES *HIGH-SPEED DRILLS* TO CREATE DELICATE *FILIGREE PATTERNS* ON OSTRICH EGGS THAT TAKE UP TO 400 HOURS TO COMPLETE!

CERAMIC SPANIELS ARE THE TRADITIONAL WEDDING GIFT TO MINERS IN SO. WALES, IN THE BELIEF THEY *WILL GUARD HIS HOME AND KEEP HIM SAFE IN HIS HAZARDOUS WORK*

BELIEVE IT OR NOT! THE *LONE STAR BREWERY* IN SAN ANTONIO, TEXAS, DISPLAYS ELABORATE PORTRAITS AND MOSAICS *MADE FROM THOUSANDS OF RATTLE-SNAKE RATTLES.*

"EDIBLE ART"

ROLAND WINBECKLER OF KENT, WASH., CREATES LIFE-SIZE SCULPTURES— *INCLUDING MARILYN MONROE, KING TUT AND HUGE LIONS AND TIGERS—* OUT OF SUGAR, FLOUR, SHORTENING AND BUTTER CREAM!

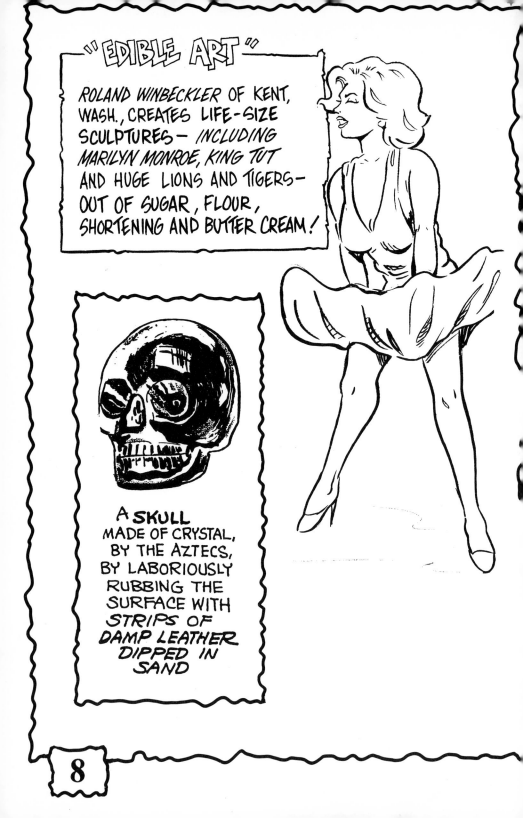

A **SKULL** MADE OF CRYSTAL, BY THE AZTECS, BY LABORIOUSLY RUBBING THE SURFACE WITH *STRIPS* OF *DAMP LEATHER DIPPED IN SAND*

Fun

IN ORDER TO COPYRIGHT THEIR MAKEUP DESIGNS, *CIRCUS CLOWNS* PAINT FACES ON *EGG SHELLS* AND THE SHELLS ARE KEPT *INSIDE VAULTS* AT THE INTERNATIONAL CIRCUS CLUB *IN PARIS!*

ROGER BOUCKAERT OF BELGIUM WORKED 5 HOURS A DAY FOR 4 YEARS TO CREATE A CROSSWORD PUZZLE THAT HAD OVER 50,000 *WORDS* AND WAS 30 *METERS* LONG!

IN RALEIGH, N.C., FANS OF STAR TREK ARE ORGANIZING THE ONLY PLANNED COMMUNITY IN THE WORLD WHERE FOLLOWERS CAN *LIVE OUT THE MORAL CODE SET DOWN BY THE POPULAR TELEVISION SHOW!*

IN JULY 1989, 1,200 PEOPLE PLAYED MONOPOLY CONTINUOUSLY FOR 50 DAYS *WHILE SUBMERGED IN A 30,000-LITER TANK OF WATER,* IN ATLANTA, GA.!

LEN ASHTON, A SOUTH AFRICAN CIRCUS PERFORMER, CAN BALANCE HEAVY OBJECTS ON HIS CHIN—*INCLUDING A LAWN MOWER, A CHAIR HOLDING HIS 3-YEAR-OLD SON AND A WASHING MACHINE!*

AMERICAN CHARLEY LANG HAS COMPLETELY COVERED THE WALLS AND CEILINGS OF HIS HOUSE WITH OVER 1,000,000 JIGSAW PUZZLE PIECES!

EUGENE SANDOW, A 19TH CENTURY STRONGMAN, COULD TEAR THREE FULL DECKS OF CARDS *IN HALF!*

CATHERINE DE MEDICIS, QUEEN OF FRANCE, *CREATED THE FIRST MAJORETTES* WITH A TROUPE OF YOUNG WOMEN WHO PERFORMED AT THE COURT OF THE LOUVRE IN THE 16TH CENTURY!

MICHAEL LAUZIERE, AN ENTERTAINER FROM MONTREAL, CANADA, CAN SQUEEZE HIS ENTIRE BODY *INSIDE A GIANT, INFLATED BALLOON—THEN POP IT WITH A PIN!*

FOR 37 YEARS, RESIDENTS OF CAWKER CITY, KAN., HAVE BEEN WINDING *HAY TWINE* INTO A BALL THAT NOW MEASURES 40 FT. 3 IN. IN DIAMETER AND WEIGHS 14,984 LBS.!

REBECCA SMITH OF SALEM, ORE., THE WORLD'S ONLY *FEMALE HUMAN CANNONBALL*, IS REGULARLY SHOT A DISTANCE OF 110 FT. AT A SPEED OF 40 MPH—FROM A CIRCUS CANNON!

Ripley's — Believe It or Not!®

Games

WORLD CHESS CHAMPION GARRI KASPAROV, WHO HAS WON *EVERY* TOURNAMENT SINCE 1981, RECENTLY DEFEATED *"DEEP THOUGHT,"* A CHESS COMPUTER, IN THE *WORLD COMPUTER CHESS CHAMPIONSHIP* IN NEW YORK CITY, N.Y.!

EIGHTEENTH-CENTURY FRENCH COMPOSER AND CHESS MASTER *FRANCIS ANDRÉ DANICAN* WAS THE FIRST MAN TO WIN A GAME OF CHESS WHILE *BLINDFOLDED!*

*O*NCE EVERY TWO YEARS, IN MAROSTICA, ITALY, A CHESS GAME IS PLAYED ON A HUGE BOARD WITH PEOPLE DRESSED IN 15ᵀᴴ CENTURY COSTUMES ACTING AS THE CHESS PIECES.

IN NOVEMBER, 1989, THE FIRST WORLD CHAMPIONSHIP OF *NON SNOOKER* WAS HELD AT THE TYBURN CONVENT IN LONDON, ENGLAND!

BRITISH PRIME MINISTER NEVILLE CHAMBERLAIN (1869-1940) INVENTED THE GAME OF SNOOKER.

EDDY McDONALD OF TORONTO, CANADA, A WORLD RECORD **YO-YO CHAMP,** IN DECEMBER 1989, PERFORMED 7,962 LOOP-DE-LOOPS IN LESS THAN AN HOUR!

A **DART GAME** PLAYED IN FRANCE IN THE EARLY 1900s, HAD THE CONTESTANTS THROWING THREADED NEEDLES

IN ASHLAND, WIS., IT IS AGAINST THE LAW TO PLAY MARBLES FOR KEEPS!

IN 1975, FROM JUNE 25TH THROUGH JULY 25TH, GEORGIA CHAFFIN AND TAMMY ADAMS OF CULLMAN, ALA., PLAYED ON A SEESAW FOR 730 1/2 HOURS!

Ripley's Believe It or Not!®

Hobbies

B.W. CRAWFORD OF DENTON, TEXAS, CREATES SCULPTURES OF SUCH FAMOUS FIGURES AS *ELVIS*, *DOLLY PARTON* AND *MISS PIGGY — USING PECAN SHELLS!*

GEORGE GUTARRA OF *NEW YORK CITY, N.Y.*, CREATES SCULPTURES FROM PIECES OF STAINLESS STEEL CUTLERY!

BILL BROWNLEE OF PRAIRIE VILLIAGE, KAN., IS A MEMBER OF THE *INTERNATIONAL BRICK COLLECTORS* WHOSE 375 MEMBERS ARE DEDICATED TO "STIMULATING INTEREST IN THE COLLECTION OF *BRICKS.*"

NORMAN KAUTZ, A MACHINIST IN TEXAS CITY, TX , BUILDS MODEL SHIPS *INSIDE LIGHTBULBS!*

DEBORAH LACAYO OF COTTAGE GROVE, ORE., CARVES AND PAINTS MINIATURE PEOPLE ON THE ENDS OF TOOTHPICKS!

REG POLLARD OF MANCHESTER, ENGLAND, BUILT A 13-FT.-LONG REPLICA OF A 1907 "SILVER GHOST" ROLLS ROYCE USING 63 PINTS OF GLUE AND 1,016,711 *MATCHSTICKS.*

Ripley's Believe It or Not!®

Movies and Movie Stars

ACTOR **JohnWayne**, WHO WAS BORN MARION MICHAEL MORRISON IN 1907, WAS NAMED "DUKE" AFTER HIS PET AIRDALE!

HORROR FILM STAR BELA LUGOSI WAS BURIED IN HIS FAVORITE 'DRACULA' CAPE!

The Movies

THE GORILLA IN THE 1930's FILM **KING KONG** WAS NOT A HUGE MECHANICAL CREATURE BUT *AN 18-IN. HAND-HELD MODEL !*

THE LONGEST FILM EVER SHOWN WAS A 1970 BRITISH FILM THAT *RAN FOR 48 HOURS* CALLED "THE LONGEST, MOST MEANINGLESS MOVIE IN THE WORLD"!

DURING WORLD WAR II THE OSCAR AWARDS WERE MADE OF WOOD DUE TO A SHORTAGE OF METAL !

DURING THE 1976 FILMING OF "KING KONG," A 40-FT.-TALL APE MADE OF "STYROFOAM" AND HORSEHAIR WAS DROPPED 110 STORIES FROM NEW YORK CITY'S WORLD TRADE CENTER.-

IN JAPAN, GODZILLA MOVIES ARE NOT ALLOWED TO BE FILMED AT THE OSAKA AIR-PORT OR NEAR TOKYO'S IMPERIAL PALACE.-

ACTRESS GRETA GARBO (1905-1990) MADE HER SCREEN DEBUT IN AN ADVERTISING FILM CALLED "HOW NOT TO WEAR CLOTHES!"

ASTOR
SEAN CONNERY, FAMOUS FOR THE ROLE OF *JAMES BOND*, ONCE HAD A JOB AS A COFFIN POLISHER!

ACTRESS *LILLIAN GISH* PLAYED LIONEL BARRYMORE'S DAUGHTER IN AN EARLY SILENT FILM, HIS WIFE IN A 1930s FILM AND HIS MOTHER IN THE 1947 FILM, *"DUEL IN THE SUN!"*

SINCE THE MOVIE "FIELD OF DREAMS" WAS RELEASED IN 1989, OVER 10,000 PEOPLE HAVE VISITED THE DIAMOND THAT WAS CREATED FOR THE FILM IN A CORNFIELD NEAR DYERSVILLE, IOWA!

CHARLIE CHAN, THE FICTIONAL CHINESE DETECTIVE CREATED BY EARL DERR BIGGERS, *WAS NEVER PORTRAYED IN THE MOVIES BY A CHINESE ACTOR!*

THE FIRST MOTION PICTURE TO BE COPYRIGHTED IN THE UNITED STATES WAS OF A *MAN SNEEZING.!*

THE EPITAPH ON THE TOMBSTONE OF *MEL BLANC*, THE MAN OF 1,000 VOICES INCLUDING BUGS BUNNY, PORKY PIG AND DAFFY DUCK READS: *"THAT'S ALL FOLKS!"*

BELIEVE IT OR NOT! THE ROLE OF SHERLOCK HOLMES *HAS BEEN PLAYED* BY 69 DIFFERENT ACTORS IN 194 FILMS!

MARILYN MONROE WAS THE INSPIRATION FOR "BATMAN'S" GIRL FRIEND VICKI VALE!

"GRAVE LINE", A COMPANY IN *LOS ANGELES, CA,* TAKES TOURISTS ON A TOUR OF *THE GRAVES* OF SUCH HOLLYWOOD STARS AS MARILYN MONROE, MONTGOMERY CLIFT AND DOUGLAS FAIRBANKS — IN A HEARSE!

ACTOR **WALTER BRENNAN** (1894-1974) STARTED HIS CAREER IN HOLLYWOOD BY DOING *A VOICE-OVER FOR A DONKEY!*

COMEDIAN **W.C. FIELDS** ONCE WORKED AS A *PROFESSIONAL DROWNER* — REGULARLY PRETENDING TO DROWN IN ORDER TO DRAW CROWDS TO THE BEACH IN ATLANTIC CITY!

AMERICAN FILMMAKER ARMANDO ACOSTA IS DIRECTING AN ADAPTION OF SHAKESPEARE'S ROMEO & JULIET — WITH 1 HUMAN ACTOR AND 120 CATS!

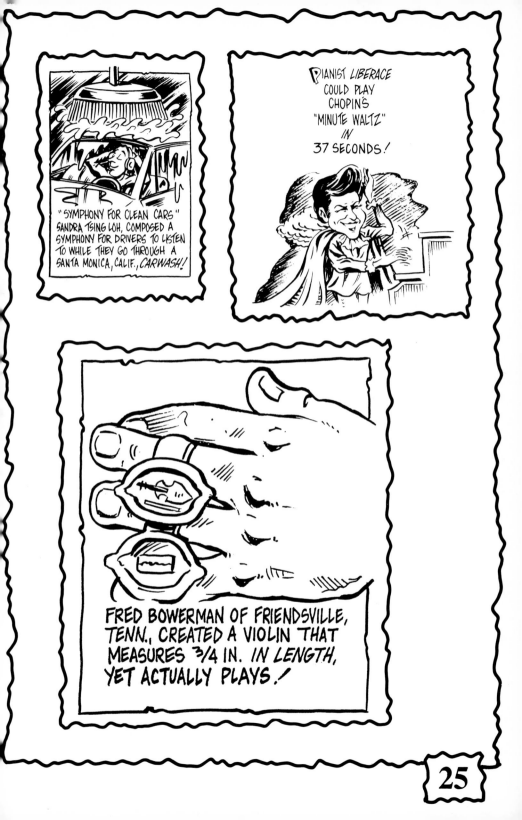

"SYMPHONY FOR CLEAN CARS" SANDRA TSING LOH, COMPOSED A SYMPHONY FOR DRIVERS TO LISTEN TO WHILE THEY GO THROUGH A SANTA MONICA, CALIF., *CARWASH!*

PIANIST *LIBERACE* COULD PLAY CHOPINS "MINUTE WALTZ" *IN* 37 SECONDS!

FRED BOWERMAN OF FRIENDSVILLE, TENN., CREATED A VIOLIN THAT MEASURES 3/4 IN. *IN LENGTH,* YET ACTUALLY PLAYS!

Ripley's ——Believe It or Not!®
Music and Dance

IRVING BERLIN
(1888-1989)
THE AMERICAN COMPOSER OF "WHITE CHRISTMAS" SOLD HIS *FIRST* SONG IN 1907 FOR **37** CENTS!

IN THE 18TH CENTURY, MISS DARNETT, "THE SINGING STRONG LADY," SUPPORTED A PLATFORM WITH A PIANO AND SANG A SONG WHILE A PIANIST ACCOMPANIED HER!

HENRY ALBAN CHAMBERS, THE ORGANIST AT LEEDS CATHEDRAL IN YORKSHIRE, ENGLAND, IN 1913, WAS ONLY 11 YEARS OLD!

AN ANSWERING MACHINE IN SAN DIEGO, CALIF., CREATED TO TAKE CALLS FROM "ELVIS SPOTTERS," HAS ALREADY RECEIVED OVER 50,000 CALLS!

GEORGE COOK OF BRAMPTON, ONT., CANADA, HAS COMPOSED 120,000 SONGS, OVER 60,000 OF THEM IN THE LAST 4 YEARS!

IN 1925, AMERICAN COMPOSER GEORGE ANTHEIL CAUSED A RIOT IN A PARIS THEATER USING *XYLOPHONES, A FIRE SIREN* AND *HIGH-SPEED PLANE PROPELLERS* IN A PERFORMANCE OF HIS "BALLET MÉCHANIQUE"!

IN 1990, THE FRENCH GOVERNMENT CREATED A NEW CABINET POSITION CALLED *MINISTRY OF ROCK AND ROLL!*

BILL PETTAWAY OF *ANNAPOLIS, MD,* COMPOSER OF "*MILLI VANILLI'S*" HIT SONG "**GIRL YOU KNOW IT'S TRUE**," IS A *MILLIONAIRE* WITH 26 GOLD RECORDS—YET HE REFUSES TO QUIT HIS *DAY JOB PUMPING GAS!*

A U.S. JET PILOT CAN BE TRAINED IN 13 *MONTHS*, BUT IT TAKES 15 *MONTHS* FOR A BANDMASTER TO TRAIN AT THE PENTAGON'S SCHOOL OF MUSIC!

ACCORDING TO SOME *INDIAN MUSICIANS*, IT TAKES *150 YEARS*, OR *SEVERAL INCARNATIONS*, FOR A PERSON TO MASTER THE ART OF *PLAYING THE SITAR!*

ENGLISH COMPOSER VAUGHAN WILLIAMS (1872-1958) WROTE A CONCERTO FOR THE *HARMONICA.*

THE TAITO CORP. OF JAPAN HAS DEVELOPED THE *FIRST ROBOTIC ORCHESTRA* WITH AN ELECTRONICALLY CONTROLLED VIOLIN, PIANO *AND* FLUTE!

ARNIE STRYNADKA OF GOODFISH LAKE, CANADA, CREATED A MUSICAL INSTRUMENT *FROM A HOUSEHOLD PLUNGER* WITH AN ELECTRONIC PICK UP THAT IS PLAYED WITH A COAT HANGER!

BELIEVE IT OR NOT! THERE ARE OVER 4,000 POPULAR SONGS IN WHICH THERE ARE REFERENCES *MADE TO ROSES!*

AT THE SHIKISHIMA BAKING CO. IN JAPAN, BAKERS IMPROVE THE TASTE OF THEIR BREAD *BY PIPING CLASSICAL MUSIC INTO THE DOUGH!*

IN 1954 WHEN ROSA PONSELLE (1897-1981) TRIED TO MAKE A RECORDING WITH RCA, HER VOICE *SHATTERED THE RECORDING EQUIPMENT!*

PETE, A PIT BULL TERRIER, MAKES $250 A DAY BY BARKING IN TIME TO THE MUSIC OF THE ROCK BAND, 'PJ AND THE MAGIC BUS.'

IN APRIL 1990, A GUITAR OWNED BY JIMI HENDRIX WAS SOLD AT AN AUCTION FOR THE RECORD PRICE OF **$355,000**!

IN 1967, *HEINZ ARNT* OF DUSSELDORF, GERMANY, PLAYED THE PIANO FOR 44 DAYS— OR 1,054 HOURS—*WITHOUT STOPPING*!

OPERA SINGER ENRICO CARUSO PRACTICED SINGING TWICE A DAY WHILE TAKING A BATH WITH A PIANIST ACCOMPANYING HIM IN THE NEXT ROOM.—

THE FAMOUS POLISH PIANIST, *PADEREWSKI* (1860-1941), HAD EACH OF HIS FINGERS SEPARATELY INSURED.

TOP 40
VIVALDI
PHIL COLLINS
DAVID BOWIE

ANTONIO VIVALDI'S 18TH CENTURY WORK, *"THE FOUR SEASONS,"* EDGED OUT **PHIL COLLINS** ON THE BRITISH HIT PARADE IN 1990!

"THE WORLD'S BEST-SELLING SINGER"

LATA MANGESHKAR OF INDIA HAS RECORDED *OVER 30,000 SONGS* SINCE 1948 AND HAS SOLD 2 *BILLION* RECORDS—MORE THAN ELVIS OR MICHAEL JACKSON!

RUSSIAN COMPOSER **SERGEI PROKOFIEV** CREATED HIS OPERA "**THE GIANT**" AT THE AGE OF **9**!

IN 1969, *MALCOLM FOGIN* COMPOSED A "SOLO FOR DOUBLE BASS" *WHICH, IF PLAYED, WOULD GO ON FOR* 73,000,000,000 YEARS!

JAPANESE WOMEN IN THE 1880s WORE SANDALS WITH AIR-FILLED BELLOWS IN THEIR HEELS THAT PRODUCED MUSICAL NOTES WHEN WORN!

BELIEVE IT OR NOT.✓ "HYDRODAKTULPSYCHICHARMONICA" IS THE NAME FOR A MUSICAL INSTRUMENT THAT CONSISTS OF *AN ARRANGEMENT OF GLASSES!*

BELIEVE IT OR NOT.✓ SALFORD COLLEGE OF TECHNOLOGY IN ENGLAND OFFERS A DEGREE IN POP MUSIC *WITH JOHN LENNON SCHOLARSHIPS!*

SHIRLEY MAE ROSS OF ROCKVILLE, MD, TAUGHT HER PET SCHNAUZER TO *PLAY THE PIANO!*

In 1987, at the Edmonton, Canada, Heritage Festival, 10,442 people danced in a giant *CONGA LINE.*

A record 5,271 tap dancers performed a choreographed routine as a tribute to the late SAMMY DAVIS JR. in New York City in 1990.

IN RIO de JANEIRO, IT'S AGAINST THE LAW *TO DANCE THE SAMBA INSIDE OF A TUNNEL!*

IN 1990, IN COLUMBUS, OHIO, **910** PEOPLE DANCED THE *"HOKEY POKEY"* IN A GIANT CIRCLE *IN THE OUTFIELD* OF COOPER STADIUM!

COMPOSER AND PIANIST *FREDERIC CHOPIN (1810-1849)* OFTEN WORE A BEARD *ON ONLY ONE SIDE OF HIS FACE—* THE SIDE FACING THE AUDIENCE.

IN 1929, OTTO E. FUNK WALKED 4,165 MILES IN 183 DAYS — FROM NEW YORK CITY TO SAN FRANCISCO — *PLAYING A FIDDLE THE ENTIRE TIME!*

THE GREAT RUSSIAN PIANIST VLADIMIR HOROWITZ

WOULD PERFORM ONLY ON SUNDAYS AT 4 P.M., ATE NOTHING BUT CHICKEN AND SOLE, AND *TAUGHT HIS STUDENTS WHILE HE LAY ON THE FLOOR!*

ON THE 1930s, ARTHUR LLOYD OF MEDFORD MA, "THE HUMAN CARD INDEX," CARRIED 15,000 CARDS IN 40 POCKETS, AND *COULD LOCATE ANY CARD IN 5 SECONDS!*

RUSSIAN REVOLUTIONARY *LEON TROTSKY,* ONCE APPEARED AS AN EXTRA IN A *HOLLYWOOD MOVIE.*

THE COMPOSER *LUDWIG* van *BEETHOVEN* (1770-1827) FREQUENTLY POURED ICE WATER OVER HIS HEAD *TO STIMULATE HIS BRAIN.*

ARGENTINE CONTORTIONIST HUGO ZAMARATTE CAN FOLD HIS 5 FT. 9 IN. FRAME *INTO A BOTTLE* 26 INCHES HIGH AND 18 INCHES WIDE!

BELIEVE IT OR NOT! GEORGE UHRIN OF MISSOURI CITY, TEXAS, CAN MEMORIZE 1,560 PLAYING CARDS— IN THEIR EXACT ORDER!

IN 1989, KOLYA VASIN, AN ELVIS PRESLEY FAN IN LENINGRAD, WAS ISSUED A VISA TO THE U.S. FOR THE SOLE PURPOSE OF VISITING PRESLEY'S HOME, GRACELAND!

GRACELAND OR BUST!

SINGER CARA ALDINI ONCE RENTED NEW YORK'S CARNEGIE HALL TO SING DUETS WITH HER *PET GOOSE!*

BELIEVE IT OR *NOT!* IN CARYVILLE, FLA., THERE IS AN ANNUAL INTERNATIONAL WORM FIDDLING CONTEST IN WHICH CONTESTANTS PLAY MUSIC TO DRAW *EARTHWORMS OUT OF THE SOIL!*

BELIEVE IT OR *NOT!* ALFRED *HITCHCOCK* (1899-1980) DID NOT HAVE A *BELLYBUTTON!*

YOGI BAIRD OF HOUSTON, TX, IS A **CONTORTIONIST** WHO CAN PLAY THE FIDDLE WITH BOTH LEGS *TUCKED BEHIND HIS HEAD!*

FELIPE CARBONELL OF LIMA, PERU, TOLD 8,000 JOKES *IN 5 DIFFERENT LANGUAGES FOR 100 HOURS!*

BELIEVE IT OR NOT...

IN THE 1890s, WILLIAM LE ROY, A VAUDEVILLE PERFORMER CALLED **"THE HUMAN CLAW HAMMER"** COULD EXTRACT LARGE SPIKES FROM A 2-INCH PLANK—*USING HIS TEETH!*

THE **BRIDE** AT A GYPSY WEDDING IN ITALY TRADITIONALLY SMASHES A POTTERY JAR OVER THE GROOM'S HEAD

MAC NORTON, A EUROPEAN MUSIC HALL PERFORMER KNOWN AS "THE HUMAN AQUARIUM," SWALLOWED GOLDFISH AND LIVE FROGS!

IN 1923, SIEGMUND BREITBART, A POLISH STRONGMAN, DROVE A 20-PENNY NAIL THROUGH *THREE* ONE-INCH BOARDS AND *FIVE SHEETS* OF GALVANIZED IRON-- USING ONLY HIS FIST!

WILLIAM ELSWORTH ROBINSON, A 19th CENTURY CONJUROR, *PERFORMED A TRICK IN WHICH HE CAUGHT **BULLETS** IN A PLATE!*

ACTOR JAMES EARL JONES, THE VOICE OF DARTH VADER IN "STAR WARS," STUTTERED SO BADLY AS A CHILD THAT HE HAD TO COMMUNICATE BY WRITING NOTES!

"THE MIGHTY ATOM"
JOE GREENSTEIN, A NEW YORK CARNIVAL STRONGMAN IN THE 1930s, COULD BITE A 20-PENNY NAIL AND A 25-CENT PIECE — IN TWO.

COMEDIAN BOB HOPE WAS A BOXER BEFORE HE BECAME AN ENTERTAINER.

JAMES JARVIS OF STRATFORD, ONT., CANADA, RECEIVED A $47,000 PIANO AS A GIFT FOR ANSWERING A NOTE HE FOUND *INSIDE A BOTTLE!*

IN 1989, GALEN SHINKLE OF RINGOLD, GA, SHOT 10 BULL'S-EYES AT A 6-INCH DISK IN 60 SECONDS *WHILE SUSPENDED UPSIDE-DOWN FROM JOE PONDER'S TEETH!*

45

FRANKLY, PANSY...

JUST DAYS BEFORE IT WAS PUBLISHED IN 1936, THE ORIGINAL NAME FOR THE CHARACTER OF *SCARLETT O'HARA* IN THE NOVEL "GONE WITH THE WIND" WAS *PANSY!*

IN THE 1930s HOLLYWOOD MAKEUP ARTIST **MAX FACTOR** INVENTED A HAND-OPERATED *KISSING MACHINE* WITH RUBBER MOLDED LIPS THAT WERE PRESSED TOGETHER TO TEST *LIPSTICK!*

ANNA PAVLOVA,

THE GREAT RUSSIAN BALLERINA, PLAYED POKER TO RELAX, AND ONCE *CHOREOGRAPHED A DANCER'S STRIKE* DURING THE OCTOBER REVOLUTION!

JIM GARY OF FARMINGDALE, N.J., CREATES FULL-SCALE SCULPTURES OF DINOSAURS — INCLUDING A 47-FT.-LONG *DIPLODOCUS* AND A 24-FT.-LONG *TYRANNOSAURUS REX* OUT OF OLD CAR PARTS!

JACK LANNOM, A KUNG-FU EXPERT FROM FT. LAUDERDALE, FLA., *CAN SMASH 2,400 LBS. OF ICE WITH A SINGLE BLOW OF HIS HAND!*

BELIEVE IT OR NOT, ! IN FEB., 1990, ENTERTAINER *TERRY COLE* BALANCED **16 CRATES** ON HIS CHIN FOR *16 SECONDS!*

IN APRIL 1990, FOUR ASTEROIDS DISCOVERED BY MEMBERS OF THE INTERNATIONAL ASTRONOMICAL UNION WERE DEDICATED AND NAMED AFTER *EACH OF THE FOUR BEATLES!*

IN THE 1923 CECIL B. DEMILLE FILM *THE TEN COMMANDMENTS,* **BLOCKS OF JELLO** CARVED INTO WAVES WERE USED FOR *THE PARTING OF THE RED SEA!*